If Sarah Will Take Me

If Sarah Will Take Me

Poem by Dave Bouchard
Paintings by Robb Terrence Dunfield

ORCA BOOK PUBLISHERS

Many people have touched my life but I wouldn't be the person I am today without the belief and support from my Mom and Dad, brothers and sisters, and my wonderful wife, Sarah.
R.T.D.

How not? … For you Robb!
D.B.

Autumn Landscape

If I could walk,
I'd walk down to the ocean
I'd kick off my sandals
And I'd walk on the sand.

I'd start in the morning,
In the cool of the morning,
I'd walk through mid-day,
When sand turns to coal.
You'd see me at sunset,
Alone on the beaches,
Near a handful of lovers,
And I'd be walking on air.

And though I can't walk,
I can cherish the memories
Of sand in my toes,
Of my weight on the mud.

And if Sarah will take me,
I'll show you the place
Where I'd kick off my sandals
And walk on the sand.

A Walk on the Beach

If I could breathe
On my own when I chose to,
I'd go to a dock
Where I'd stood as a boy.

I'd be there at daybreak
For the smell of the ocean,
And still at mid-day
Taking deep, heavy breaths.
You'd see me at sunset,
Still standing there breathing,
By a few lonely trawlers,
Wanting more and more air.

And though I can't breathe
On my own as I use to,
I can still smell the ocean
That's been for all time.

And if Sarah will take me,
I'll show you the place
Where I'd stand on the dock,
Where I'd go just to breathe.

West Coast Drydock

If I could move
Any way that I chose to,
I'd go to a dam
That I've not seen for years.

I'd get there at sunrise
When the grass is still soaking.
I'd perch on the rail
That hangs over the lake.
Come noon I'd climb back
To the table we ate on,
And sit like an Indian
Until it got late.
I'd move back to the grass
And lie under the stars,
With my hands 'neath my head —
Just me and the sky.

And though I can't sit
Or stretch out as I once did,
I can cherish the memories
Of that time in my life.

And if Sarah will take me
To that dam of my childhood,
I'll paint you my memories
Of that time long ago.

Saturday Afternoon at the Dam

If I could ski,
Not the way that I once did,
Just stand on my feet
And slide down a hill.

I'd take out my parka,
And head for the mountains.
I'd race for the top
For a place in the clouds.
I'd leave off my toque
And go without glasses.
I'd worship the wind
And the sun on my face.
I'd be certain to stop
And look back every minute,
At my tracks down the hill
Where I'd moved through the snow.

And though I can't ski,
I can cherish the memories
Of flying down the slopes,
With my face in the sky.

And if Sarah will take me,
I'll show you the place
That rekindles this passion
That just will not die.

Downhill Run

If I could throw
And catch as I once did,
I'd go to a field
Where I played long ago.

I'd go all alone,
Again in the morning,
Head into the sun
And I'd start on my own.
I'd run from one tree
Across to the other,
And back to the first one —
I'd run till I dropped.
And if someone passed by
In the late of the evening,
They'd question the footsteps
That they heard in the dark.

And though I can't throw
And catch as I once did,
I can cherish the memories
Of playing on that field.

And if Sarah will take me
To what once was my childhood,
I'll paint you the reason
That I still yearn to play.

Spring Creek in the Morning

If I could lift
My arms to my shoulders,
I'd not turn to nature,
I'd turn to my home.

I'd go to my mother
And hold her so tightly
She'd not dare to move.
She'd stand still in my arms.
I'd then find my father,
My brothers and sisters,
And reach for the touch
That we knew long ago.

And though I can't lift
My arms to my shoulders,
I can still feel their warmth.
I am never alone.

And if Sarah will take me
To a place near the meadow,
I'll paint you the reason
That I long for my arms.

Picking Apples in Autumn

If I had the chance
To live my life over,
To start from my birth
Or go back a few years.
Like most, there is much
That I'd try to do better.
Like you there are things
That I'd do differently.

Reflections

I've made some mistakes,
The kind that you learn from,
I've paid for them all
Though *one was too dear!*
And yet through the years
I've learned to see both sides:
It's left me with less,
And it's made me much more.

Challenging Life's Elements

It's made me more caring
Of those closest to me.
It's brought me much closer
To nature's front door.
It's highlighted small things
That I'd not even noticed.
It's made me look inward.
I have no place to hide.

Picking Spring Flowers

If I could share
My soul with all children
(I wake every day
Wanting yet to do more),
I'd tell them a story
Of simple and fun things,
Of playing on the beach
On the sea's open floor.
I'd tell them to cherish
Each day as it happens,
Through colours and music,
A soft touch or a smile.

You Can if You Believe You Can

And the key to my message
In sharing this passion
Is to have them all see
The man I've become.

Sandy Cliffs

And if Sarah will take me,
I'll go out and find them.
I'll reach out and show them
My world deep inside.

And for those that I miss,
I'm right *here* in my paintings,
The fruits of my labour,
The joy of my life.

Afternoon in the Garden

Church by the Sea

Writing *If Sarah Will Take Me* was difficult because my tears kept getting in the way.

I had asked Robb for pictures of his family to help me try to see and feel the way he must have felt then and now. I sat at my computer surrounded by these images ... trying to write these feelings ... his feelings ... constantly having to pause for the tears.

I had met Robb seven years earlier when he came to speak to the students at the high school where I worked. I knew him to be a popular motivational speaker who had been a ventilator-dependent quadriplegic since he was nineteen. His goal was to share his message with as many young people as he could reach. I also knew Robb to be from a large, loving family, and I had heard of his passion for sport and the outdoors.

I listened to him speak of the youthful sense of invincibility that preceded his fall from an uncompleted second-floor balcony during what was otherwise a fairly ordinary teen party. I thought that I might be able to help Robb reach a larger audience with his message. Thus, the birth of *If Sarah Will Take Me*.

Sarah was one of the nurses working for Robb and his five roommates in what was the world's first independent-living complex for such high-level injured as Robb and his friends. Robb and Sarah were married in 1992 and shortly after moved into their own home.

Today Robb continues his intensive motivational speaking program. He has, however, spent most of his time over the past decade painting. His art now resides in many corporate and private collections and draws significant attention from enthusiasts worldwide.

The publisher would like to acknowledge the ongoing financial support
of the Canada Council, the Department of Canadian Heritage and the
British Columbia Ministry of Small Business, Tourism and Culture.

Canadian Cataloguing in Publication Data
Bouchard, Dave, 1952–
If Sarah will take me

ISBN 1-55143-081-9
1. Dunfield, Robb Terrence, 1959—Poetry. 2. Physically handicapped—
Poetry. I. Dunfield, Robb Terrence, 1959– II. Title.
PS8553.O759I45 1997   C811'.54   C96–910788–9   PR9199.3.B617I45 1997

Library of Congress Catalog Card Number 96-72451

Design by Christine Toller
Printed and bound in Hong Kong

Orca Book Publishers
PO Box 5626, Station B
Victoria, BC   V8R 6S4
Canada

Orca Book Publishers
PO Box 468
Custer, WA 98240-0468
USA

99 98 97   5 4 3 2 1